# Behavioral Economics and the Stock Market

Roggie Clark

# Continue Learning At Our Website: Roggieclarkbooks.com

Continue exploring educational resources, tools, books, workbooks, and learning materials designed to help readers continue building knowledge and practical skills. Visit: www.roggieclarkbooks.com

Inside you'll find:

- Educational worksheets
- Beginner-friendly guides
- Printable activities
- Companion materials for books and courses

A growing library of educational content for readers, collectors, learners, parents, teachers, and lifelong students.

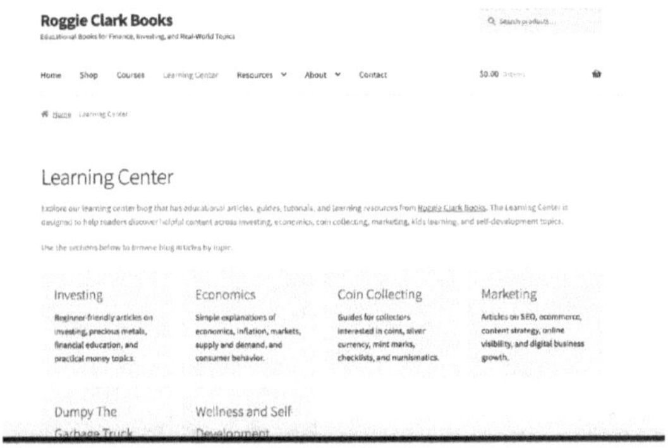

# The Strategic Guide to U.S. Mint Gold and Silver Coin Investing

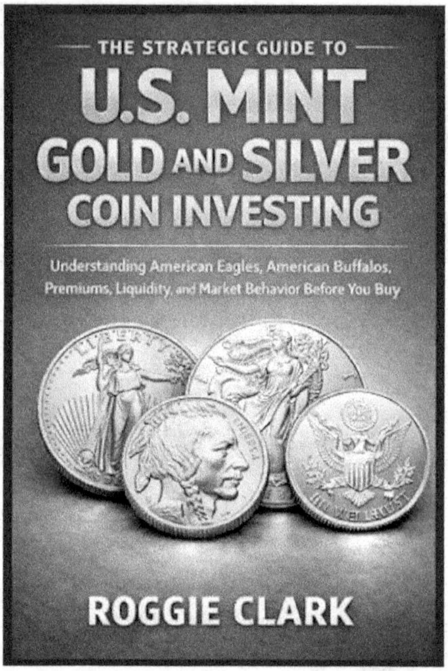


Rather than offering a general introduction to precious metals, this guide examines how American Gold Eagles, American Gold Buffalos, and Silver American Eagles behave in real investor markets.

https://www.amazon.com/Strategic-Guide-U-S-Silver-Investing/dp/B0GQKJF9K6

# Copyright

Title: Behavioral Economics and the Stock Market
Author: Roggie Clark



Cover Design: Roggie Clark
Editing: Renee' Clark

Printed in the United States of America

# Disclaimer

The views and opinions expressed in this publication are those of the author and do not necessarily reflect the official policies, positions, opinions, or viewpoints of any individual, company, organization, institution, agency, or entity referenced or mentioned within this work.

The author is not necessarily affiliated with, endorsed by, sponsored by, or compensated by any individuals, companies, organizations, brands, institutions, products, or services referenced within this publication unless specifically stated otherwise. Any examples, sample situations, stories, illustrations, or scenarios presented may be fictionalized or simplified for educational purposes. Any resemblance to actual persons, living or dead, businesses, or events is purely coincidental unless otherwise stated.

The information, ideas, strategies, concepts, techniques, opinions, suggestions, and educational materials contained in this publication are provided on an "as is" basis without warranties of any kind, either express or implied. While every effort has been made to provide accurate and current information, neither the author nor the publisher makes any representations or warranties regarding the completeness, accuracy, reliability, suitability, or applicability of the information presented.

This publication is intended solely for educational and informational purposes and should not be interpreted as professional advice of any kind, including but not limited to financial, investment, legal, tax, business, medical, mental health, educational, psychological, or other professional guidance. Readers should conduct their own independent research and consult appropriately qualified professionals before making decisions that may affect their finances, health, business, education, legal matters, personal circumstances, or other important areas of life.

Results, outcomes, and experiences may vary significantly among individuals. Neither the author nor the publisher guarantees any specific outcomes, results, earnings, performance improvements, personal achievements, or benefits resulting from the use of information contained in this publication.

By reading, accessing, or using this publication, you acknowledge and agree that the author and publisher shall not be held liable for any direct, indirect, incidental, consequential, financial, personal, emotional, or other damages, losses, or claims arising from the use, misuse, interpretation, or application of information contained within this publication. You assume full responsibility for any actions, decisions, and outcomes resulting from the use of this material.

## Image Credits and Public Domain Notice

All images, illustrations, graphics, photographs, visual references, and related materials included in this publication are believed to be in the public domain, used under applicable licenses or permissions, created by the author or publisher, or obtained from sources that clearly identify them as available for lawful use.

The author and publisher have made a good faith effort to use only visual materials that are lawfully available for use and distribution. Where applicable, images and visual materials may have been resized, cropped, edited, enhanced, stylized, modified, reformatted, or arranged for educational, informational, design, formatting, or presentation purposes.

This publication is intended for educational, informational, and illustrative purposes only. The inclusion of any image, artwork, photograph, visual reference, symbol, historical material, design, or graphic element is not intended to claim ownership over public domain materials or any third-party intellectual property rights that remain with their respective owners.

If you believe any image or visual material included in this publication has been used in error, please contact the author or publisher so the matter may be reviewed and corrected in future editions or releases if necessary.

Any factual information, specifications, historical references, values, descriptions, statistics, or related content accompanying visual materials are provided for general informational purposes only and may change over time. Readers should conduct their own independent research and consult appropriate sources or qualified professionals when making decisions based on information presented in this publication.

This publication is independently produced and is not affiliated with, endorsed by, sponsored by, or associated with any company, organization, government agency, institution, trademark holder, or third party unless specifically stated otherwise.

# Table of Contents

# Introduction: Markets Are Made of People

Financial markets are often discussed through numbers. Prices rise and fall, companies report earnings, interest rates change, funds move capital, and investors compare risk with expected returns. These measurements are important, but they can make the market appear more mechanical than it really is. Behind the numbers are people making decisions. Retail investors decide whether to buy, sell, hold, or move their money somewhere else. Portfolio managers decide how billions of dollars should be allocated. Asset owners decide which managers receive capital. Analysts form expectations, investment committees debate risk, and institutions respond to changing market conditions. The stock market may operate through securities and prices, but those prices ultimately reflect the decisions of market participants.

## Behavioral Economics and Financial Markets

Traditional economics gives us a useful starting point for understanding those decisions. An investor has limited resources and different ways to allocate them. Each choice presents potential benefits, costs, and risks. A rational investor should evaluate those alternatives and choose the one expected to provide the greatest utility based on the investor's preferences and constraints.

There is nothing wrong with beginning there. The rational investor gives us a benchmark against which actual behavior can be examined.

The difficulty is that real investors do not make decisions with perfect information about the future. They do not know exactly where interest rates will be next year, what a company's future earnings will be, or how millions of other investors will respond to tomorrow's news. Even when investors have access to good information, they still have to interpret it.

This is where **behavioral economics** becomes useful. Behavioral economics examines how psychological, cognitive, emotional, and social influences can affect economic decisions. Instead of assuming that people always process information perfectly and consistently choose the option that maximizes their interests, behavioral economics examines what happens when actual human behavior enters the decision.

Imagine an investor considering a stock that has increased substantially over the previous year. The investor can study the company's financial statements, valuation, expected earnings, and competitive position. But the investor may also know that friends have made money from the stock. Financial media may be discussing it constantly.

The investor may regret not buying six months earlier and fear missing another increase.

The financial information still matters. What has changed is the way the investor is interpreting the opportunity.

The same issue appears when prices fall. An investor may become anchored to the price originally paid for a stock and resist selling because accepting the lower price makes the loss feel more real. Another investor may see the same decline and become increasingly afraid of losing even more money. Both investors observe the same market price, yet their responses can be very different.

Concepts such as **loss aversion**, anchoring, overconfidence, herd behavior, framing, and social proof help us examine why.

Behavioral economics does not require us to assume that every unexpected decision is irrational. A decision that initially appears irrational may reflect incentives or preferences that were missing from the original model. An investor who refuses to sell during a downturn may have a long time horizon. A fund manager who holds a position may face constraints that an outside observer cannot see. An institution that follows a benchmark may be responding to its mandate rather than simply copying other investors.

The goal is therefore not to replace economic analysis with psychology. It is to recognize that economic decisions are being made by people.

That distinction also applies to professional investors.

Financial institutions may have sophisticated models, experienced analysts, extensive data, and professional risk-management systems, but the people inside those institutions still make judgments. Portfolio managers can become overconfident. Analysts can become anchored to earlier expectations. Investment committees can reinforce existing beliefs. Managers can feel pressure when competitors outperform them.

Professional investors also operate under incentives that are different from those facing someone investing personal savings. A portfolio manager may consider expected returns and risk while simultaneously thinking about benchmark performance, investor withdrawals, reputation, compensation, investment mandates, and career consequences.

Institutional behavior is therefore not simply retail investor behavior with more money. The incentives and constraints can be very different, even though both ultimately involve human decision making.

## From Individual Decisions to Market Activity

The behavior of one investor usually means very little to the overall stock market. If one person becomes frightened and sells $2,000 of stock, the broader market will barely notice.

The economic significance changes when many people begin making similar decisions.

Suppose a market has been rising for several years. Investors see strong recent returns. Financial coverage becomes increasingly positive. People who previously stayed out of the market begin seeing friends, coworkers, professional investors, and financial commentators discussing the gains. Some investors become concerned that waiting means missing an opportunity.

More money enters the market. Rising demand can contribute to higher prices. Those higher prices produce additional gains, and the gains attract additional attention.

The market itself has now become part of the behavioral environment.

Investors are no longer responding only to earnings, valuations, or economic conditions. They are also responding to the behavior and results of other market participants.

This can create a **behavioral feedback loop**. Market activity affects investor expectations, those expectations influence decisions, and those decisions create new market activity.

The same basic process can work during falling markets. Declining prices can change perceptions of risk. Investors who were comfortable holding assets during a rising market may suddenly become much more concerned about losses. Some sell. Other investors observe the selling and falling prices. Their own expectations may change.

None of this means psychology alone determines stock prices. Earnings, interest rates, inflation, liquidity, leverage, economic growth, government policy, and countless other factors can influence markets.

Behavior can interact with those conditions.

A weak economic environment may create legitimate reasons for investors to become more cautious. Behavioral responses can then influence how strongly and how quickly market participants react to that information.

This distinction becomes especially important when thinking about bubbles and crashes. A market crash should not automatically be explained as investors becoming irrational. Financial crises can involve credit problems, excessive leverage, liquidity shortages, economic shocks, and structural problems. Behavioral economics instead gives us a way to ask how people respond once those pressures appear, and whether those responses amplify or reduce the movement already underway.

Individual behavior becomes economically important when individual decisions begin to aggregate.

## Institutional Investors, Retail Investors, and the Movement of Capital

The stock market contains many types of participants, but two groups will receive particular attention throughout this book: **retail investors** and **institutional investors**.

Retail investors are individuals investing their own money. They may purchase stocks directly, hold exchange-traded funds, invest through mutual funds, contribute to retirement accounts, or participate in markets through other investment products.

Institutional investors operate on a much larger scale. The category can include mutual funds, hedge funds, pension funds, insurance companies, endowments, asset managers, and other organizations responsible for investing substantial pools of capital.

The distinction is useful, but the relationship between the two groups is not always simple.

Consider a retail investor who puts $10,000 into a mutual fund. The retail investor makes the decision to allocate money to the fund, but the investor does not decide which individual securities the fund purchases. That responsibility belongs to the fund's investment professionals.

Two layers of decision making now exist.

The investor decides where to place the capital.

The investment manager decides how to invest it.

If many investors add money to or withdraw money from funds, those decisions create **fund flows**. Investment managers may then have to respond to changes in available capital and liquidity. Their responses can contribute to buying and selling activity in financial markets.

The relationship can also move in the opposite direction. Institutional activity can influence prices, financial news, market sentiment, and expectations. Retail investors observe those changes and may alter their own decisions.

Asset owners add another layer. Pension plans, endowments, foundations, and other large capital owners may allocate money among different investment managers. Their decisions can create significant changes in where capital is being managed and how it eventually enters financial markets.

This gives us a much broader view of market behavior.

A retail investor may react to a market decline. A mutual fund may experience investor withdrawals. An investment manager may respond to changing fund flows. An asset owner may reconsider an allocation. Other institutions may respond to price movements or changing expectations. Those decisions can interact rather than occurring independently.

This is why **capital flows** will be so important throughout this book.

Human behavior by itself does not move a market. Decisions do.

Once those decisions involve buying, selling, allocating, redeeming, or repositioning capital, psychology can become economic activity.

At sufficient scale, that activity can influence markets. The resulting market conditions then become new information for the people making the next round of decisions.

That interaction is at the center of what we are going to explore.

# Last Thoughts

The stock market is not simply a collection of prices, companies, and financial assets. It is also a system of interacting decision makers. Retail investors, institutional investors, asset owners, portfolio managers, and other participants respond to information, incentives, risk, expectations, and one another. Behavioral economics gives us a framework for examining the human side of those decisions, while traditional economics helps us understand the incentives and market forces surrounding them. The important question is not whether markets are driven by economics or psychology. Human behavior is part of economic activity. What becomes particularly interesting is what happens when individual decisions begin interacting, capital begins moving, and the behavior of one group of market participants starts influencing the behavior of another.

# Chapter 1: The Economics of Investor Decision Making

Every investment decision begins with a choice. An investor can buy one asset instead of another, keep money in cash, accept additional risk in pursuit of a higher expected return, or decide that a potential reward is not worth the uncertainty involved. Traditional economics gives us a structured way to examine these choices through preferences, constraints, incentives, and utility. Behavioral economics does not require us to abandon that framework. Instead, it allows us to examine what happens when real people make these decisions with incomplete information, uncertain expectations, and their own perceptions of risk.

## Rational Choice, Utility, and the Traditional Investor

Traditional economic theory generally begins with the idea that people make choices based on their preferences and the resources available to them. An investor with $50,000 cannot place the same $50,000 into every available investment at once. Choosing stocks means giving up some opportunity to hold bonds, cash, real estate, or another asset.

Even choosing one stock means giving up the opportunity to place that capital into another stock. Every allocation therefore involves an opportunity cost.

Within this framework, **rational choice** describes the idea that an individual evaluates available alternatives and chooses the option expected to best satisfy their preferences. In economics, the satisfaction or benefit associated with a choice is often described as **utility**. This is important because investors are not necessarily trying to maximize the same thing.

It is easy to assume that every investor simply wants the highest possible return. If that were true, investment decisions would be much easier to model. In reality, investors may care about return, but they can also care about liquidity, stability, income, diversification, taxes, time horizon, and the possibility of losing capital. An investor may willingly accept a lower expected return if doing so reduces exposure to a level of risk that the investor considers unacceptable.

Imagine two investors considering the same portfolio. The first investor is investing money that will not be needed for several decades. The second expects to use the money for a major purchase next year. A sharp temporary decline may be inconvenient for the first investor but financially disruptive for the second. The investment has not changed. What has changed are the preferences and constraints of the person evaluating it.

This is why utility gives us a better starting point than simply assuming that investors want the greatest number of dollars possible. Two investors can examine the same potential return and assign very different value to it because they also evaluate what must be risked to obtain that return.

The traditional investor can therefore be thought of as someone making tradeoffs. Higher expected returns may come with greater uncertainty. Greater liquidity may come with lower expected returns. Concentrating a portfolio may increase exposure to a successful investment while also increasing the consequences of being wrong. The investor considers these tradeoffs and chooses according to their preferences.

This framework is useful precisely because it gives us something against which actual behavior can be compared. If we observe an investor making a choice that appears inconsistent with the traditional model, we can begin asking why. Perhaps the model is missing an important preference or constraint. Perhaps the investor has different information. Or perhaps the investor is interpreting the choice in a way that the traditional model does not fully capture.

Behavioral economics becomes particularly useful when we reach that third possibility.

# Risk, Uncertainty, and How Investors Evaluate Choices

Investment decisions are unusual because the decision is made in the present while much of the outcome exists in the future. An investor can study what a company earned last year, but the investor is purchasing a claim on what the company may produce in the years ahead. Historical information can inform that decision, but it cannot remove uncertainty about what comes next.

This gives us an important distinction between **risk** and **uncertainty**. Risk generally describes situations in which probabilities can be estimated or modeled. Uncertainty goes further because the probabilities themselves may be difficult to know. Financial markets contain both.

An investor can study historical volatility and estimate how much a portfolio has fluctuated in the past. Historical data may also help estimate how different assets have behaved under certain economic conditions. These calculations can be useful for thinking about risk. But no historical dataset can tell an investor exactly what technologies will emerge, which companies will fail, what geopolitical events will occur, or when an unexpected financial crisis will begin.

The investor therefore has to make decisions without knowing the complete range of future outcomes.

Traditional economics can approach this problem through **expected utility**. Instead of simply asking which investment has the highest possible return, the investor considers possible outcomes, the likelihood of those outcomes, and how much value each outcome provides. This helps explain why an investor might reasonably choose a more stable investment even when another alternative offers greater potential returns.

But there is another problem. Investors do not experience risk only as a mathematical probability. They also perceive it.

Consider a stock market that has risen steadily for several years. Investors have repeatedly watched declines recover and portfolios increase in value. A person who has experienced mostly positive returns may gradually become more comfortable taking risk. The market can begin to feel safer even though uncertainty about the future has not disappeared.

Now imagine the market falls sharply. Portfolio values decline, financial news becomes negative, and discussions about recession or financial instability become more common. The same investor may suddenly view stocks as considerably more dangerous.

The underlying concept of risk did not appear overnight. What changed was the investor's perception of it.

This distinction between actual risk and **perceived risk** matters because investors make decisions based on what they believe could happen. Those beliefs can be influenced by experience, information, expectations, and recent events. An investor who recently experienced a severe loss may evaluate the same investment differently from someone who has only experienced rising markets.

Professional investors face this problem as well. Institutional investors may have sophisticated risk models and access to far more information than most individuals, but models still require assumptions. Portfolio managers must decide which risks deserve attention, how much uncertainty they are willing to tolerate, and what conditions would justify changing a position.

The institutional setting can also change how risk is evaluated. A fund manager may believe an investment remains attractive over five years while simultaneously worrying that investors will withdraw capital after six months of underperformance. An asset owner may have a long-term objective but still reconsider a manager after several disappointing years. Risk can therefore involve more than the probability that an asset declines. It can include liquidity needs, investor behavior, performance expectations, and institutional constraints.

This is one reason financial decision making cannot be reduced to a simple calculation of expected return. Investors are choosing among uncertain futures, and they have to decide which risks matter to them before those futures are known.

## Where Behavioral Economics Changes the Model

Behavioral economics becomes important when we compare the traditional model with the decisions people actually make. The goal is not to declare that investors are irrational whenever their choices surprise us. Instead, behavioral economics asks whether systematic features of human behavior can help explain decisions that are difficult to understand through the traditional model alone.

Imagine an investor purchases a stock for $100 per share and later watches the price fall to $70. From a purely forward-looking perspective, the original $100 purchase price should not determine whether the investor continues owning the stock. The relevant question is what the investor expects from the stock at its current price compared with the available alternatives.

But people do not always think that way.

The investor may begin thinking about getting back to $100. Selling at $70 feels like accepting the loss, while continuing to hold leaves open the possibility of recovering it. The original purchase price has become psychologically important even though it does not determine the stock's future value.

This is where behavioral concepts begin adding something to the economic model. Anchoring can make a previous price unusually influential. Loss aversion can make accepting a loss feel more significant than an equivalent gain. The investment decision still involves economics, but the way the investor experiences the available choices may differ from what a simple rational model predicts.

Success can influence behavior too. Suppose another investor makes several profitable investments in a row. The investor may reasonably conclude that some of those decisions were good, but repeated success can also increase confidence beyond what the evidence supports. The investor may begin taking larger positions, trading more frequently, or placing greater weight on personal judgment. A successful outcome has now influenced the behavior surrounding the next decision.

This raises an important distinction between the quality of a decision and the quality of its outcome. A carefully researched investment can lose money because the future is uncertain. A poorly researched investment can make money because favorable events occur. Judging the original decision only by the eventual return can therefore teach investors the wrong lesson.

Markets make this especially difficult because gains and losses provide constant feedback. An investor who makes money after taking excessive risk may interpret the profit as proof that the strategy was sound. A portfolio manager who makes a carefully reasoned contrarian decision and temporarily underperforms may face pressure to abandon it. Outcomes can influence future behavior even when those outcomes do not tell the complete story about the original decision.

Other market participants create another layer. Investors rarely make decisions without knowing something about what other people are doing. Rising prices, falling prices, trading activity, analyst expectations, fund performance, and financial commentary all provide information about the actions and beliefs of others.

Sometimes that information is valuable. If investors respond to a meaningful change in a company's prospects, observing their behavior may tell us something about how the new information is being interpreted.

The behavioral problem appears when the behavior of others begins replacing independent evaluation. An investor may buy because everyone appears optimistic. A portfolio manager may become uncomfortable avoiding a popular sector because competing funds are outperforming. An asset owner may direct additional capital toward a manager largely because that manager recently produced unusually strong returns.

The decision may still have a rational explanation. The manager may have genuinely superior information or skill. The popular sector may have stronger fundamentals. The crowd may be correct.

Behavioral economics does not require the crowd to be wrong.

Instead, it asks why people joined the crowd and how the behavior of others affected their choices.

This is particularly important in financial markets because decisions eventually become transactions. A belief that remains inside someone's head does not directly move capital. A decision to buy, sell, allocate, or redeem does.

Once enough investors make similar decisions, individual behavior can begin producing larger economic effects. What begins as a personal judgment about risk or return can become part of a broader movement of capital.

That connection between individual decision making and collective market activity is one of the reasons behavioral economics matters so much to the study of financial markets.

## Last Thoughts

Traditional economics gives us a foundation for understanding investor decision making through preferences, constraints, utility, risk, and uncertainty. Behavioral economics builds on that foundation by examining how real people interpret those choices. Investors do not simply calculate outcomes. They experience gains and losses, remember previous prices, form expectations from incomplete information, respond to uncertainty, and observe what other market participants are doing. The important point is not that investors are either rational or irrational. Investment decisions can contain elements of both careful economic reasoning and human behavioral influence at the same time. Understanding that interaction gives us a stronger foundation for examining the retail investor, where these behavioral influences become especially visible in decisions involving losses, recent market experiences, and the behavior of the crowd.

# Chapter 2: Psychology and the Retail Investor

Retail investors make financial decisions in an environment where information is widely available but certainty is impossible. An investor can study earnings, valuations, economic conditions, historical returns, and company performance, but eventually a decision still has to be made about an uncertain future. That decision is not made by a mathematical model. It is made by a person who remembers previous gains and losses, has expectations about what might happen next, watches other market participants, and experiences the consequences of being right or wrong. This is where behavioral economics becomes particularly useful. It helps us examine how the psychology of the retail investor can influence decisions that eventually become actual movements of capital.

## Loss Aversion, Reference Points, and the Fear of Losing

Imagine two investors who own the same stock at the same current price of $70. The first investor purchased the stock for $100. The second purchased it for $40. From this point forward, both investors own exactly the same asset and face the same future possibilities. Psychologically, however, their positions may feel completely different. One investor sees a $30 loss, while the other sees a $30 gain.

The difference comes partly from the point against which each investor measures the outcome. A **reference point** is the position an individual uses to evaluate whether an outcome feels like a gain or a loss. In the stock market, the original purchase price is an obvious reference point, but investors can create others. A previous portfolio high, an expected return, the performance of the S&P 500, or even another person's investment performance can become the standard against which an investor evaluates results.

This matters because people do not necessarily experience gains and losses equally. **Loss aversion** describes the tendency for losses to have a greater psychological impact than equivalent gains. An investor who gains $5,000 may be pleased, but losing that same $5,000 can produce a much stronger emotional response. The numbers may be equal, but the experience of those numbers is not necessarily symmetrical.

Now return to the investor who purchased a stock for $100 and watches it fall to $70. Instead of asking whether the stock is still an attractive investment at $70, the investor may begin thinking about getting back to $100. Selling at $70 means accepting the loss. Holding the stock preserves the possibility that the original investment will eventually recover.

The problem is that the market does not know what the investor originally paid. The future return of the stock depends on what happens from its current price forward. If the investor would not purchase the stock at $70 today, continuing to own it primarily because it once traded at $100 introduces a behavioral consideration into what might otherwise be a forward-looking economic decision.

Loss aversion can also produce behavior that appears contradictory. An investor may initially refuse to sell a declining investment because realizing the loss feels painful. If the price continues falling, however, the fear of experiencing an even larger loss can eventually become stronger than the desire to recover the existing one. The investor who refused to sell at the beginning of the decline may later become desperate to get out.

This is one reason investor behavior during market downturns can change so quickly. People are not simply reacting to a percentage displayed on a screen. They are continually reevaluating what the loss means and what they believe could happen next.

There is also an important difference between imagining a loss and experiencing one. An investor might comfortably say that a portfolio could withstand a 20 percent decline. That statement is easier to make while the market is rising. When the decline actually happens, the investor may be watching years of accumulated gains disappear while simultaneously hearing about layoffs, recession risks, declining earnings, and other investors selling.

The investor's financial circumstances may not have changed, but the perception of the decision can change dramatically. A theoretical willingness to accept risk is now being tested by an actual loss.

This does not mean that selling during a decline is irrational. New economic information may justify the decision. A company's prospects may have deteriorated. An investor's financial needs may have changed. The broader economy may be weakening. Behavioral economics is not an argument for ignoring legitimate information simply because fear is present. It gives us a way to examine whether the reaction to that information is being influenced by the psychological experience of losing.

## Anchoring, Recency, and the Information Investors Remember

Retail investors face another problem: there is far more information available than any individual can process completely. A person researching a company can encounter earnings reports, analyst estimates, historical prices, valuation ratios, interest-rate expectations, economic data, management commentary, financial news, social media discussions, and opinions from other investors. Some information has to receive more attention than other information.

That creates opportunities for mental shortcuts to influence judgment.

We have already seen how anchoring can make an original purchase price unusually important. The same tendency can influence the way investors interpret many other numbers. Suppose a stock traded at $150 last year and now trades at $90. An investor may immediately view $90 as inexpensive because the stock used to trade much higher.

But the previous price alone tells us very little about whether the stock is currently undervalued. The company's expected earnings may have declined. Its competitive position may have weakened. Economic conditions may have changed. The original $150 price may itself have been excessive. It is also possible that the stock really has become inexpensive. The point is that $150 should not become evidence of value simply because investors remember seeing the stock at that price.

Previous market highs can function similarly. An investor who sees an index substantially below its former peak may assume that returning to that peak is inevitable. An analyst's earlier price target can continue influencing expectations even after the assumptions behind the target have changed. A previous interest rate can become the level people expect rates to eventually return to. Once a number becomes established in the mind, it can continue influencing judgments even when circumstances have changed.

Investors can also place disproportionate importance on whatever happened most recently. **Recency bias** can cause recent events or experiences to carry greater weight when people form expectations about the future. After several years of strong stock market performance, investors may gradually begin treating strong returns as normal. After a severe downturn, those same investors may begin treating another decline as increasingly likely.

Neither expectation necessarily follows from the recent experience.

Consider someone who begins investing during a long bull market. Most of that investor's personal experience may involve temporary declines followed by recoveries and new highs. Risk can begin to feel abstract because taking risk has repeatedly been rewarded. Another person who begins investing shortly before a major crash may develop a very different understanding of what owning stocks feels like.

Both investors can study the same historical data. Their personal experiences can still influence how they interpret it.

This connects with the **availability heuristic**, where information that is easy to remember can receive greater weight in judgment. Dramatic events are especially available to memory. Investors remember crashes. They remember stocks that increased several hundred percent. They remember spectacular corporate failures and extraordinary success stories.

Ordinary periods are less memorable.

Financial media can reinforce this imbalance because unusual events naturally receive more attention. A market moving a fraction of a percent on an ordinary day does not generate the same attention as a sudden collapse. The events investors hear about most frequently are therefore not necessarily the events that occur most frequently.

This matters because investors have to turn information into expectations. If recent or memorable information receives too much weight, expectations about the future can become heavily influenced by a relatively small part of the available evidence.

The effect becomes even more important when expectations lead to action. An investor who believes recent strong returns will continue may increase exposure to stocks. Another who remains focused on a previous crash may hold substantially more cash. Their beliefs have now become allocation decisions.

Once capital moves, the behavioral effect is no longer limited to what an investor thinks.

## Herd Behavior, Social Proof, and FOMO

Investors do not only interpret financial information. They also observe other investors interpreting it. This creates an unusual environment in which the behavior of other people can itself become information.

Suppose a stock begins rising rapidly. At first, relatively few people pay attention. As the price continues increasing, the stock receives more coverage. Investors begin discussing it online. Friends talk about the money they have made. Analysts revise expectations. Professional investors disclose positions. The continued rise attracts even more attention.

Someone who previously had no interest in the company may eventually begin wondering whether staying out of the investment is a mistake.

This is where **FOMO**, or fear of missing out, can influence financial decisions. The investor may still care about the company's fundamentals, but another consideration has entered the decision. Other people appear to be making money, and the investor is not participating.

The behavior of others can also create **social proof**. When people are uncertain about what to do, they sometimes look at what others are doing for information. This is not automatically unreasonable. Other market participants may possess information or expertise that an individual investor does not have. Observing their actions can therefore provide useful information.

The difficulty comes when investors begin responding primarily to one another rather than to the underlying information.

Imagine one investor buys because a company's prospects have improved. Another sees the price increase and buys because the market appears optimistic. A third notices that more investors are entering and interprets the increased demand as confirmation that the investment is attractive. More people join because they see others making money.

Eventually, the behavior can develop into **herd behavior**, where investors increasingly move in the same direction partly because other investors are already moving in that direction.

This does not mean the herd must be wrong. If a company develops a highly profitable new product and its expected future earnings increase dramatically, thousands of investors may independently reach the reasonable conclusion that the company has become more valuable. Large numbers of people making the same decision are not proof of irrationality.

The more interesting behavioral question is why each investor made the decision. There is a meaningful difference between purchasing an asset because its economic prospects improved and purchasing it because everyone else appears to be purchasing it.

Financial markets make this distinction difficult because prices themselves can influence behavior. In many ordinary markets, a higher price discourages demand. If the price of a household product doubles, consumers may look for alternatives. In financial markets, a rapidly rising price can sometimes attract additional buyers because the increase is interpreted as evidence that the asset is desirable.

A rising price attracts attention. Attention can attract investors. Additional investors create additional demand. That demand can contribute to further price increases, which attracts even more attention.

The market has now become part of the behavioral process.

The same process can operate in reverse. Falling prices attract negative attention. Investors see other people selling and begin wondering what those sellers know. Continued declines make losses increasingly visible. Some investors who were willing to hold at the beginning of the decline become less comfortable as they observe more people leaving.

Once again, this does not mean that selling is irrational. The underlying economic situation may genuinely be deteriorating. The behavioral question is whether the behavior of other investors is amplifying the response.

Retail investors are also watching institutions. A well-known fund taking a position can be interpreted as evidence that sophisticated investors see an opportunity. Institutional selling can create the opposite impression. At the same time, professional investors are watching retail sentiment, market prices, fund flows, and the behavior of other institutions.

This means there is not simply one crowd in the stock market. Different groups of market participants can watch and respond to one another.

That interaction is important because retail decisions can eventually become institutional considerations. An individual investor may decide to move money into a mutual fund after seeing strong recent performance. Thousands of investors making similar decisions can create substantial inflows. The investment manager now has additional capital to manage. If investors begin withdrawing instead, the fund experiences outflows.

A psychological response has become a financial flow.

This is where the distinction between individual behavior and market behavior begins to narrow.

One investor experiencing FOMO is primarily a personal behavioral event. Large numbers of investors responding similarly can move substantial amounts of money.

The next question is what happens when that money reaches institutions.

## Last Thoughts

Retail investor psychology does not operate separately from economics. Loss aversion can change how investors experience declines, reference points can affect how gains and losses are evaluated, and recent or memorable information can influence expectations about the future. Investors also observe one another, allowing social proof, FOMO, and herd behavior to become part of financial decision making. None of these tendencies means retail investors are inherently irrational, and following other investors is not automatically a mistake. Their importance comes from what happens when behavioral responses become actual decisions. Buying, selling, investing, and withdrawing move capital. When many individual decisions begin moving in similar directions, retail investor psychology can become part of a much larger financial process. The next step is to examine the other side of that interaction: the institutions and professional decision makers responsible for managing large pools of capital.

# Chapter 3: The Human Side of Institutional Investing

Institutional investors are often treated as the more sophisticated side of financial markets. They employ professional portfolio managers, analysts, economists, traders, and risk specialists. They may have access to extensive research, large datasets, specialized technology, and financial models that most retail investors could never reproduce on their own. Those advantages matter, but they do not remove human behavior from the investment process. Institutions do not literally make decisions. People working within institutions make decisions while responding to mandates, incentives, performance expectations, organizational pressures, and the expectations of the people whose capital they manage. Behavioral economics therefore remains relevant even when the decision maker is responsible for millions or billions of dollars.

## Institutional Investors, Asset Owners, and Investment Managers

The term institutional investor covers many different types of organizations. Mutual funds, hedge funds, pension funds, insurance companies, endowments, and other large investment organizations can all participate in financial markets, but they do not necessarily have the same objectives. A mutual fund managing money contributed by thousands of investors operates differently from a pension fund investing assets intended to support future retirement obligations. A hedge fund may have a different strategy, investor base, risk tolerance, and investment mandate from either of them.

This is why it is useful to distinguish institutional investors from **asset owners** and **investment managers**. An asset owner ultimately owns, controls, or represents a pool of capital. A pension plan, endowment, foundation, or other organization may decide how much of its capital should be allocated to stocks, bonds, private investments, or other assets. The asset owner may manage some investments internally while hiring outside investment managers to manage others.

An investment manager occupies a different position. The manager receives responsibility for investing capital according to an agreed strategy or mandate. Within the investment organization, portfolio managers and analysts then make more specific decisions about how that capital should be allocated.

This creates several layers of decision making. Imagine a pension fund decides that 20 percent of its portfolio should be managed using a particular equity strategy. The pension fund selects an outside asset manager. The asset manager receives the capital, and a portfolio manager decides which securities should be held within the strategy. The original decision about where capital should go and the eventual decision about which stock should be purchased are connected, but they are not the same decision.

The distinction becomes important when behavior enters the process. Suppose the investment manager underperforms for several years. The asset owner may begin questioning whether the manager should continue receiving the allocation. If the asset owner withdraws the capital, that decision changes the amount of money the investment manager has available to manage. The manager may then need to adjust the portfolio.

In this case, market activity can begin before anyone makes a new judgment about the underlying stocks. The initial decision concerns who should manage the money. That decision changes the location of the capital, which can eventually affect investment activity.

Retail investors can create a similar relationship through mutual funds and other investment products. A retail investor decides whether to place money into a fund. The fund manager decides how the pooled capital should be invested. If the retail investor later withdraws the money, another decision enters the process.

The investor and manager therefore have different responsibilities. One decides where capital should be managed, while the other decides how that capital should be invested.

This also means that professional investors are rarely operating with complete freedom. A portfolio manager may have strong opinions about the market but still be required to follow a particular mandate. A fund designed to invest primarily in large U.S. companies cannot simply move the entire portfolio into cash or foreign bonds because the manager becomes uncomfortable with stock valuations. An investment manager must operate within the purpose for which the capital was provided.

Understanding institutional behavior therefore requires us to understand the structure surrounding the decision maker. The question is not simply what the manager believes will happen. We also have to ask what the manager is responsible for doing, what constraints exist, and who is evaluating the results.

## Incentives, Benchmarks, Performance Pressure, and Career Risk

Consider a portfolio manager who believes a particular investment strategy will perform extremely well over the next ten years but may underperform the broader market for the next two. If the manager were investing only personal money, accepting two years of weak relative performance might be relatively straightforward. The manager could simply wait for the long-term thesis to develop.

Managing other people's capital changes the situation.

Clients and asset owners may not be willing to wait ten years. They can compare the manager's performance with competitors, market indexes, and other investment opportunities. If the strategy underperforms for long enough, capital may leave before the manager's long-term expectation has an opportunity to be proven correct.

This is where institutional incentives become important. A manager is not evaluated only on whether an investment eventually makes money. Performance can be evaluated relative to time horizons, risk limits, mandates, competitors, and benchmarks.

A **benchmark** provides a reference against which investment performance can be compared. This can be extremely useful. A 5 percent return tells us relatively little by itself. If comparable investments lost 10 percent during the same period, that return may appear impressive. If the relevant market gained 20 percent, the same 5 percent return looks very different.

Benchmarks can therefore improve the way performance is evaluated, but they can also affect behavior. A manager who builds a portfolio that differs substantially from the benchmark creates the possibility of significant outperformance. The manager also creates the possibility of significant underperformance.

Suppose a manager believes a popular sector has become significantly overvalued and reduces exposure to it. The sector continues rising for another year. Competing managers who maintained large positions outperform. Clients begin asking why the fund did not participate in the gains. Asset owners question the strategy. The manager may still believe the original analysis is correct, but the professional consequences of waiting have increased.

This creates **career risk**. Investment decisions can affect compensation, reputation, client relationships, advancement, and employment. These considerations become part of the environment in which professional decisions are made.

That does not mean portfolio managers simply choose whatever protects their careers. It means that the incentives surrounding professional investing can be more complicated than maximizing expected investment returns.

A manager can believe that a particular position is economically attractive while also recognizing that being wrong could produce significant professional consequences. Another manager may believe that a popular investment is overpriced while recognizing that avoiding it could create substantial relative underperformance if the price continues rising.

The behavior of other managers can therefore affect the decision.

This gives us a different way to think about institutional conformity. If many professional investors hold similar positions, it is tempting to describe them as simply following the crowd. Sometimes that may be part of the explanation. But similar institutional behavior can also result from similar mandates, benchmarks, regulations, risk models, information, or performance incentives.

Being wrong with everyone else can produce a different outcome from being wrong alone.

Imagine most large funds hold a particular group of stocks and those stocks suddenly decline. A manager who also held them can explain that the portfolio was exposed to the same market event affecting competitors. Now imagine the manager avoided those stocks, invested heavily somewhere else, and suffered a large loss while competitors performed well. The second decision may attract much more scrutiny because the manager deliberately moved away from the group.

The economic incentive is therefore not always simply to find the investment with the highest expected return. Professional investors may also have to consider the consequences of being different.

This does not make institutional investors irrational. It shows that rational behavior depends partly on the incentives we include in the analysis. If career consequences, investor withdrawals, and relative performance matter to the manager, then a model that considers only the expected return of a stock may be missing part of the actual decision.

## Bias, Herding, and Decision Making Among Professionals

Professional experience can reduce some behavioral mistakes. Investment firms can create research procedures, risk limits, investment committees, and decision-making processes designed to prevent impulsive choices. Experienced investors may also recognize behavioral tendencies that an inexperienced investor does not.

But expertise does not make human psychology disappear.

A portfolio manager can still become overconfident after a period of strong performance. Several successful investments may genuinely reflect skill, but success can also make it easier to overestimate how much of the outcome resulted from that skill. If confidence grows faster than the evidence supporting it, the manager may begin taking larger positions or becoming less receptive to information that challenges existing beliefs.

Confirmation bias can become particularly important in this environment. An analyst may spend months researching a company and developing an investment thesis. The portfolio manager approves the position, capital is committed, and the investment becomes part of the fund's reported strategy. New information then appears that challenges the original thesis.

Changing the position may be economically appropriate, but changing one's mind can become harder after time, effort, reputation, and capital have already been invested in the original decision. The professional investor is still a person interpreting information.

Institutional investors also watch one another. A manager knows which sectors are performing well, which investment styles are attracting capital, and how competing funds are positioned. Asset owners compare managers. Consultants compare strategies. Analysts watch institutional activity. Market participants continually observe the decisions of other market participants.

This creates the possibility of **institutional herding**. Professional investors may begin making similar decisions partly because they observe other professionals moving in the same direction.

Again, similarity does not automatically mean irrationality. If interest rates fall sharply, many institutions may reasonably change their valuation assumptions at the same time. If a company reports unexpectedly strong earnings, many analysts may independently increase their estimates. Shared information can produce similar conclusions without any behavioral bias being involved.

The behavioral question is whether the behavior of other institutions begins influencing decisions beyond what the underlying information supports.

Suppose a sector has been outperforming for several years. Funds with large positions in the sector report strong returns. Those returns attract investor attention and new capital. Managers with less exposure begin experiencing relative underperformance. Clients ask why their portfolios are not participating in the gains.

The manager now faces more than a valuation question. The manager must also consider what other investors are doing and what continued underexposure could mean for the portfolio, the fund, and the manager's professional position.

This introduces an element of strategic interaction into institutional investing. A professional investor may care about what an asset is worth while simultaneously thinking about what other investors believe it is worth. If the manager believes an asset is expensive but also expects other market participants to continue buying it, the investment decision becomes more complicated.

This does not mean the manager should buy an asset believed to be overvalued. It means that financial markets require participants to form expectations about the behavior of other participants.

The relationship becomes even more interesting because the people evaluating investment managers are making behavioral decisions too. Asset owners may move capital toward managers with strong recent performance. Retail investors may place additional money into funds that recently outperformed. Investors may withdraw capital from strategies that have struggled.

The manager's behavior can therefore influence investors, while investor behavior can influence the conditions facing the manager.

Imagine a fund performs extremely well. The performance attracts new investors. The fund receives additional capital. The manager now has more money to allocate. If the strategy continues performing well, additional investors may arrive.

Now reverse the sequence. A fund performs poorly. Investors withdraw money. The manager has less capital and may face different liquidity conditions. Continued weak performance produces additional concern and potentially additional withdrawals.

Neither sequence proves that behavioral bias is driving the process. Investors may have legitimate reasons for adding or withdrawing capital. Managers may have sound reasons for changing portfolios.

What matters is the interaction.

Professional investors do not operate outside human behavior simply because they have more expertise. They operate within a different behavioral and economic environment. Their decisions can be influenced by incentives, benchmarks, mandates, organizational expectations, career considerations, and the actions of other market participants.

The scale is also different. A behavioral mistake made by one retail investor may affect a relatively small amount of money. A similar judgment made inside an institution can affect millions or billions of dollars.

That is where institutional behavior becomes especially important to the larger argument of this book. The human decision remains at the center, but the amount of capital attached to that decision can dramatically increase its economic significance.

# Last Thoughts

Institutional investors bring expertise, information, technology, and professional processes to financial markets, but institutional investing is still ultimately carried out by people. Asset owners decide where capital should be managed, investment managers operate within mandates and constraints, and portfolio managers make decisions while facing benchmarks, performance expectations, client demands, and career considerations. Behavioral tendencies can exist alongside these institutional incentives rather than replacing them. Professional investors can become overconfident, reinforce existing beliefs, respond to competitors, or move with other institutions for reasons that may be behavioral, economic, strategic, or some combination of all three. Understanding this human side of institutional investing prepares us for the next part of the discussion: what happens when the decisions of retail investors, asset owners, and investment managers begin moving capital through the financial system.

# Chapter 4: Capital Flows and the Behavioral Feedback Loop

Investor behavior becomes especially important to financial markets when a decision causes capital to move. A retail investor may decide to contribute money to a mutual fund, withdraw from an investment, or move capital from one asset class to another. An asset owner may increase or reduce an allocation to an investment manager. A fund may receive large inflows after a period of strong performance or experience withdrawals after a period of losses. These decisions do not remain isolated from the rest of the financial system. They can change the amount of capital institutions have available to manage, influence portfolio decisions, and eventually become part of market activity. This creates a connection between individual behavior and larger market outcomes, and it is within that connection that the behavioral feedback loop becomes particularly important.

## From Investor Decisions to Fund Flows

A retail investor who purchases shares of a mutual fund is making an investment decision, but the investor is also making a capital allocation decision. The investor is choosing to place money under the management of an institution. Once that money enters the fund, the investment manager becomes responsible for deciding how it should be invested according to the fund's strategy.

If one investor contributes $10,000 to a large mutual fund, the effect on the fund may be insignificant. If thousands of investors make similar decisions, however, the result can become a substantial inflow of capital. The same process works in reverse. Individual withdrawals that appear small on their own can collectively become significant outflows.

These **fund flows** provide one of the clearest connections between investor behavior and institutional behavior. The retail investor does not need to tell the portfolio manager what securities to buy or sell. The decision to enter or leave the fund changes the amount of capital being managed.

There are many reasons investors move money. Financial needs change. Investors rebalance portfolios, respond to changing interest rates, reconsider risk, adjust retirement allocations, or move toward investments they believe offer better opportunities. These decisions can be economically reasonable and carefully considered.

Behavioral influences can operate alongside those considerations.

Suppose a fund has significantly outperformed comparable funds for several years. Strong performance attracts attention. Investors see the historical returns and begin allocating additional money to the fund. Some may have carefully studied the manager's strategy and concluded that the performance reflects skill. Others may place greater weight on the recent returns because those results are highly visible.

The same recent performance that influences expectations can therefore influence where capital goes.

This creates an important transition. Recency, social proof, or enthusiasm may begin as psychological influences, but once an investor acts on them, the result is no longer only psychological. Money has moved from one place to another.

Asset owners can create the same effect on a much larger scale. A pension fund or endowment might decide to increase an allocation to a particular investment strategy after several years of strong performance. Another may reduce an allocation to a manager that has underperformed.

These decisions may involve extensive research, committees, consultants, risk analysis, and long-term planning. But asset owners are still evaluating uncertain future outcomes using information from the past. Recent performance, expectations, institutional preferences, and the behavior of other asset owners can therefore become part of the decision.

This is one reason it is important not to treat capital flows as purely mechanical movements of money. Behind each flow is an allocation decision.

A fund experiencing an inflow is receiving the result of decisions made elsewhere in the financial system. A fund experiencing an outflow is experiencing the same process in reverse.

The behavior of the people supplying capital has now changed the environment of the people managing it.

## How Capital Flows Affect Institutional Decisions

An investment manager may determine which securities belong in a portfolio, but the amount of capital available to manage is not always under the manager's control. Investors and asset owners can add or remove money, and those changes can affect the conditions under which portfolio decisions are made.

Consider a mutual fund receiving substantial inflows. The manager now has additional capital. Depending on the fund's strategy, liquidity needs, and existing portfolio, some of that money may eventually be invested in securities.

The manager still decides where the capital should go. The inflow does not automatically determine which stocks should be purchased. But it changes the amount of money available to allocate.

Outflows can create a different set of considerations. A fund experiencing withdrawals must have sufficient liquidity to meet redemptions. A manager may already hold enough cash or liquid securities to handle normal withdrawals. If outflows become unusually large, however, the manager may need to sell assets or otherwise adjust the portfolio.

This creates an important relationship between the preferences of the investment manager and the behavior of the people supplying the capital.

Suppose a portfolio manager believes a group of stocks has become undervalued after a sharp market decline. From the manager's perspective, falling prices may represent an opportunity to purchase more shares.

The fund's investors may see the same decline differently.

They see losses.

Some become uncomfortable and withdraw money.

The manager who would prefer to buy more of the declining securities may now be dealing with outflows instead of receiving new capital. Depending on the size and structure of those outflows, the manager may have less flexibility to act on the original investment view.

The manager and the investor have responded differently to the same market event, but their decisions are connected because one provides capital to the other.

The opposite situation can also occur. Strong performance may attract substantial inflows. The manager receives additional capital at a time when the securities responsible for the strong performance may already have increased significantly in price.

This creates an interesting tension. The strategy becomes most attractive to new investors after it has performed well, even though the manager may have found some of the underlying investments more attractive before those gains occurred.

Capital can therefore arrive when prices are high and leave when prices are low.

That does not mean investors always chase performance or that fund flows always work against investment managers. It shows how the timing of investor decisions can become relevant to institutional decision making.

Asset owners can create similar effects. A large pension fund that removes hundreds of millions of dollars from an investment manager creates a very different situation from one retail investor withdrawing from a mutual fund. The scale is different, but the underlying relationship remains recognizable. The owner of the capital makes an allocation decision, and the investment manager must respond to the new amount of capital under management.

Institutional investors are therefore influenced by more than their expectations about securities. They operate within a network of mandates, liquidity requirements, investor flows, asset-owner decisions, and organizational constraints.

This helps explain why observing an institution selling a security does not necessarily tell us exactly what the institution believes about that security.

A fund can sell because the manager believes an investment has become overvalued. It can also sell because the portfolio needs liquidity, because the fund is rebalancing, because an investment mandate changed, or because capital was withdrawn.

The transaction is visible.

The complete decision behind it may not be.

That distinction becomes important when other market participants begin interpreting institutional activity.

# When Market Activity Feeds Back Into Investor Behavior

Once institutions respond to changing capital flows, their decisions become part of financial market activity. Securities are purchased or sold, portfolio allocations change, and prices respond to the combined activity of market participants.

Those market movements then become information.

Suppose strong returns attract money into a particular investment strategy. Funds following that strategy receive additional capital. Managers allocate some of the new capital into the market. Increased demand can contribute to market activity and, depending on the scale involved, support further price increases.

Those higher prices produce stronger reported returns.

Investors observe the returns.

Additional investors become interested.

More capital enters.

This is the **behavioral feedback loop**.

The sequence does not have to begin with retail investors. An institutional allocation can influence prices, which attracts attention from other institutions and retail investors. Asset owners can shift capital toward a strategy that has performed well. Managers can respond to the resulting flows. Different groups can enter the loop at different points.

What matters is that market participants are responding partly to outcomes produced by other market participants.

This does not mean the process is irrational.

Imagine a group of companies develops a technology that significantly increases expected future earnings. Institutional investors examine the information and increase their exposure. Prices rise. Retail investors examine the same developments and also decide the companies have become more valuable.

The resulting capital flows may reflect reasonable responses to changing fundamentals.

Behavioral economics becomes more interesting when the market movement itself begins affecting expectations.

Strong returns may cause investors to become increasingly confident that strong returns will continue. Rising prices attract attention, and that attention brings additional capital. Additional buying contributes to further market activity, which can reinforce the belief that the original decision was correct.

The distinction between responding to economic information and responding to the market's response to that information can gradually become less clear.

A similar process can occur during market declines.

Suppose deteriorating economic conditions initially cause stock prices to fall. Investors have legitimate reasons to revise expectations. As losses become larger, some retail investors become increasingly concerned and withdraw capital from investment funds. Asset owners may also reconsider allocations.

Institutions now operate under changing capital conditions. Some managers may need to increase liquidity or reduce positions. Their transactions become part of the broader selling occurring in the market. Prices decline further.

Those lower prices are observed by investors who have not yet acted. The continuing decline may make the economic situation appear even more dangerous. Loss aversion becomes more relevant as portfolio values fall. Recent negative information becomes increasingly prominent. Investors observe other people selling and begin wondering whether those market participants know something they do not. Some of those investors sell too.

The original market decline has now produced behavioral responses that create additional financial decisions. Those decisions affect capital flows, which can influence institutional activity, which becomes part of the market movement investors are observing.

This does not mean behavioral feedback causes every crash or even that it is the dominant force during every period of market stress. Market declines can reflect changes in earnings, interest rates, credit conditions, liquidity, leverage, economic growth, policy, and many other factors.

The behavioral perspective gives us a different question. Once a market movement begins for legitimate economic reasons, can the responses of market participants amplify it?

Sometimes they can. Sometimes the feedback also moves in the opposite direction.

A falling market may cause one investor to sell while making another investor more interested in buying. Lower prices can improve expected returns for investors who believe the underlying assets remain valuable. Institutions with available capital may view widespread selling as an opportunity rather than a warning.

Different expectations are one reason financial markets continue functioning. Every seller needs a buyer, and the two sides do not have to interpret the same information in the same way.

Behavioral feedback is therefore not a mechanical cycle that must continue indefinitely. It can strengthen, weaken, or reverse as prices, information, incentives, and expectations change.

Its importance lies in showing how different levels of financial decision making can become connected.

An investor experiences a change in expectations and moves money. That movement becomes a capital flow. An institution responds to the new financial conditions. The institution's actions become market activity. Market activity produces new prices and information. Those prices influence the expectations of investors. The process begins again.

At a small scale, this interaction may have little importance for the broader market. At a large scale, the amount of capital involved can become substantial.

This is the point where investor behavior begins becoming market behavior.

## Last Thoughts

Capital flows connect the decisions of investors with the institutions responsible for managing money. Retail investors and asset owners decide where capital should be placed, while investment managers decide how that capital should be invested. When those allocation decisions create significant inflows or outflows, they can change the conditions facing institutions and contribute to portfolio activity. That activity then becomes part of the prices, returns, and market information that investors observe when making their next decisions. The resulting behavioral feedback loop does not replace fundamentals or imply that every movement of capital is irrational. It shows how expectations, incentives, investor behavior, institutional decisions, and market activity can interact. Once these interactions occur across enough participants and enough capital, they can contribute to movements that extend well beyond the original individual decisions.

# Chapter 5: When Behavior Moves Markets

Individual investors and institutions make decisions for different reasons, under different constraints, and with different amounts of capital. Most of the time, these decisions are dispersed across the market. One investor buys while another sells. One institution becomes more optimistic while another reduces exposure. The market absorbs these differences through ordinary trading. The situation becomes more interesting when large numbers of participants begin responding in similar ways. Expectations can reinforce expectations, rising prices can attract additional demand, and falling prices can increase the desire to sell. At that point, behavior is no longer simply something occurring inside individual portfolios. It can become part of the forces influencing the market itself.

## Expectations, Momentum, and Collective Market Behavior

Financial markets are forward-looking because investors are constantly forming expectations about what assets may be worth in the future. A stock price today reflects more than what a company earned yesterday. Investors consider what they believe the company may earn next year, how quickly it may grow, what risks it faces, and how other market conditions may change.

Expectations therefore matter because investors act on them before the future arrives.

Suppose investors become more optimistic about a company's future earnings. More investors may become willing to purchase the stock at its current price. Increased demand can push the price higher even though the expected earnings have not yet occurred. The market price has changed because expectations changed.

This is normal market behavior. Investors are supposed to evaluate the future.

Behavioral economics becomes especially relevant when changing prices begin influencing those expectations.

A stock that has risen substantially may attract more attention than one whose price has remained relatively stable. Investors observe the increase and begin asking why it is happening. Some investigate the company and find economic reasons to become more optimistic. Others may interpret the rising price itself as evidence that the market knows something important.

This can contribute to **momentum**, where recent price movements are followed by continued movement in the same direction for some period. Momentum can have many possible explanations, including the gradual incorporation of information into prices. From a behavioral perspective, however, it also raises questions about how investors react to recent performance and to the behavior of other market participants.

A rising price can influence expectations. Those expectations can influence demand. Increased demand can contribute to additional price movement.

The important idea is not that every trend is behavioral. It is that the market's recent behavior can become one of the inputs investors use when deciding what the market will do next.

The effect becomes more significant when many participants begin forming similar expectations.

Consider an industry that investors believe is entering a period of unusually rapid growth. Early investors allocate capital based on their expectations about future profits. Prices rise as those expectations become more widely accepted. Analysts increase forecasts. Institutional investors increase exposure. Retail investors become more interested as the industry's performance receives greater attention.

At this point, the original economic argument and the resulting market behavior can begin reinforcing one another. Stronger expectations produce buying, while the resulting price increases appear to validate those expectations.

This is an example of **collective market behavior**. Individual decisions aggregate into a larger pattern that can influence the environment in which the next decisions are made.

Collective behavior does not require everyone to agree. Markets always contain competing expectations. Even during a powerful rally, some investors believe prices are too high. During a severe downturn, other investors believe prices have become attractive.

What matters is the balance between those decisions and the amount of capital behind them.

This is also why the distinction between retail and institutional behavior can become less clear at the market level. A price does not tell us whether the demand behind it originated with a retail investor, a pension fund, a hedge fund, a mutual fund, or another market participant. The price reflects the interaction of buyers and sellers.

Behavior becomes market behavior when enough individual decisions begin pushing in a similar direction.

## Behavioral Feedback in Bubbles and Market Rallies

A market rally does not automatically indicate a bubble. Prices can rise because companies become more profitable, economic conditions improve, interest rates change, or investors receive new information that justifies higher valuations.

A **market bubble** is more complicated. The term generally describes a situation in which asset prices rise substantially and become difficult to justify using reasonable expectations about underlying economic value. Determining when this has occurred is much easier after prices collapse than while they are still rising.

Behavioral economics helps us examine how such conditions can develop.

Imagine an asset initially rises for a legitimate reason. Perhaps a new technology creates significant economic opportunities. Companies associated with that technology are expected to grow rapidly, and investors begin allocating capital toward them.

Some companies may genuinely become much more valuable.

As prices rise, however, the gains themselves attract attention. Investors who were initially skeptical begin reconsidering. Funds with exposure to the area report strong performance. New capital moves toward those funds. Financial coverage expands. More companies become associated with the popular investment theme.

The story can gradually change.

At first, investors may be buying because expected profits increased.

Later, some may be buying because prices have increased.

This distinction is subtle but important.

Rising prices create actual wealth for investors who already own the assets. Those gains can increase confidence and make additional risk feel easier to accept. Investors who remained outside the market may experience FOMO as they watch others profit. Strong performance can attract additional fund flows, giving investment managers more capital to allocate.

The feedback loop becomes stronger.

Institutional incentives can contribute to the process as well. A portfolio manager who avoided the popular area may begin underperforming the benchmark or competing funds. Even if the manager believes valuations are becoming excessive, continued underexposure can create performance pressure.

Asset owners may also observe that managers with greater exposure are producing stronger returns. Capital can begin moving toward the strategies that have recently performed best.

None of these participants has to believe that prices will rise forever.

They only have to make decisions that continue supporting demand.

This is one of the interesting features of market behavior. An investor can believe an asset is expensive and still purchase it because the investor expects other people to continue paying higher prices. A professional manager can dislike a valuation while remaining exposed because completely avoiding the asset creates other risks.

The decision has become partly strategic.

Expectations about other market participants now matter alongside expectations about the underlying investment.

As the process continues, narratives can become increasingly important. Investors develop explanations for why previous valuation standards no longer apply, why the opportunity is unusually large, or why recent performance can continue.

Sometimes those arguments are correct. Economies change, technologies develop, and companies can grow in ways that earlier investors did not anticipate.

The difficulty is separating justified optimism from optimism that is increasingly supported by the price increases it helped create.

A bubble therefore should not be reduced to the idea that investors suddenly become irrational. It can emerge through interactions among reasonable expectations, uncertainty, social influence, institutional incentives, capital flows, and changing prices.

The behavior becomes particularly visible when the feedback that supported rising prices begins to weaken.

If new information challenges the prevailing expectations, some investors may reduce exposure. Prices stop rising as quickly or begin falling. Recent performance becomes less attractive. Investors who entered because of momentum no longer receive the same confirmation from the market.

The feedback can change direction.

The same market that encouraged optimism can begin producing uncertainty.

## Fear, Selling Pressure, and Market Downturns

Market downturns provide the opposite environment. Rising prices can reinforce optimism, while falling prices can reinforce concern.

A decline can begin for many reasons. Corporate earnings may weaken. Interest rates may rise. Credit conditions may deteriorate. Economic growth may slow. An unexpected event may cause investors to reassess risk.

The initial decline may therefore have a clear economic explanation.

Behavioral economics becomes relevant when we examine what happens after investors begin experiencing the decline.

Suppose stock prices fall 10 percent. Some investors interpret the decline as a temporary adjustment and continue holding. Others become concerned that the economic situation is worse than expected. Some see the lower prices as an opportunity and begin buying.

There is still substantial disagreement.

Now suppose the decline reaches 20 percent.

Portfolio losses are larger. Negative financial news becomes more prominent. Investors who previously said they were comfortable with volatility are experiencing that volatility directly. Previous market highs become reference points against which current losses are measured.

Loss aversion can become increasingly important.

Some retail investors begin selling or withdrawing money from funds. Those decisions create outflows. Investment managers respond according to their strategies, liquidity positions, and redemption requirements.

Institutional investors may also change their own assessment of risk. Portfolio volatility increases. Risk limits become more relevant. Asset owners reconsider allocations. Managers may reduce positions that have become too large relative to new risk estimates.

Selling pressure can therefore come from several directions at once.

This does not mean everyone is selling because of fear. One institution may sell because its risk model requires a smaller position. Another may need liquidity. A retail investor may need money for personal reasons. A hedge fund may reduce exposure because leverage has become more difficult to maintain.

Different motivations can still produce the same market action.

They sell.

When enough selling occurs, prices can fall further.

Those lower prices then become new information for everyone else.

This is where a downturn can develop its own behavioral feedback. Investors see larger losses and become more concerned. Recent negative performance receives greater attention. The behavior of other investors creates social information. Someone who had planned to hold begins wondering whether the sellers know something they do not.

Additional selling can follow.

Liquidity can make the situation more complicated. An investor may be willing to own an asset under normal conditions but become unwilling to hold it when uncertainty rises sharply. If many market participants simultaneously place greater value on liquidity, the desire to hold cash or highly liquid assets can increase.

The result can be a situation in which people are not merely deciding what they want to own. They are also deciding what they believe they can safely sell later.

This is particularly important during periods of financial stress because expectations about other people's behavior can influence current decisions. An investor who expects others to sell tomorrow may decide to sell today.

That expectation can help produce the behavior the investor feared.

This does not mean behavioral economics provides a complete explanation for market crashes. It does not. Severe downturns can involve leverage, credit failures, liquidity shortages, deteriorating fundamentals, policy mistakes, economic contractions, and structural problems within the financial system.

Behavior can interact with all of them.

A fundamental shock can cause prices to fall. Falling prices can change investor behavior. Those behavioral responses can alter capital flows and institutional decisions. The resulting market activity can intensify the original decline.

This is why market crashes can provide such a powerful example of the relationship between individual and collective behavior.

The process can also reverse.

At lower prices, some investors begin seeing opportunity rather than danger. Expected future returns may become more attractive. Institutions with available capital may purchase assets from investors who want liquidity. Economic conditions may stabilize. New information can change expectations.

The feedback loop weakens.

Eventually, buying and selling reach a different balance.

This is an important reminder that behavioral forces do not operate in only one direction. Fear can spread, but so can confidence. Herding can contribute to buying or selling. Recent performance can make investors optimistic after gains or pessimistic after losses.

Markets contain participants with different expectations, constraints, and time horizons. Those differences can eventually interrupt a behavioral trend.

The larger lesson is that market behavior emerges from interaction. A downturn is not simply millions of isolated investors becoming afraid, just as a rally is not simply millions of isolated investors becoming optimistic. Each participant observes a market that is partly being created by the decisions of everyone else.

That is what makes financial markets especially interesting from a behavioral economic perspective.

## Last Thoughts

Behavior can become economically significant when similar decisions begin occurring across enough investors and enough capital. Expectations influence investment decisions, those decisions contribute to market activity, and market activity can then influence expectations again. During rallies, this interaction can reinforce optimism, attract capital, and contribute to conditions associated with bubbles. During downturns, losses, uncertainty, changing risk perceptions, and selling pressure can create feedback in the opposite direction. None of this means behavioral economics replaces explanations involving earnings, interest rates, liquidity, leverage, credit, or economic conditions. It adds another layer to the analysis by examining how people respond to those conditions and to one another. The result is a market in which individual decisions can aggregate into collective outcomes, and collective outcomes can become part of the information shaping the next individual decision.

# Chapter 6: Understanding Markets Through Behavioral Economics

Behavioral economics gives us a broader way to think about financial markets because it connects individual decision making with the economic environment in which those decisions occur. Investors still respond to prices, incentives, risk, expected returns, and limited resources, but they also interpret information through their own expectations and experiences. Institutions add another layer because professional decision makers operate within mandates, benchmarks, organizational structures, and relationships with the people supplying their capital. When these participants interact, the stock market becomes more than a collection of isolated investment choices. It becomes a system in which the decisions of one participant can alter the conditions facing another.

## Behavioral Economics, Microeconomics, and Market Outcomes

Behavioral economics is closely connected to **microeconomics** because both are concerned with decision making. Microeconomics examines how individuals, households, firms, and other economic actors allocate scarce resources and respond to incentives. Behavioral economics expands that analysis by examining how people actually make those choices when psychological and cognitive influences are present.

The connection is especially useful in financial markets. An investor has limited capital and must decide how to allocate it. Choosing one investment creates an opportunity cost because the same money cannot simultaneously be allocated somewhere else. The investor also has preferences involving risk, return, liquidity, time horizon, and other considerations. These are familiar microeconomic problems.

Behavioral economics does not replace them. Instead, it changes some of the assumptions we make about how the decision occurs. An investor may have a clear financial objective but still become anchored to a previous price. Another may understand diversification but become overconfident after several successful investments. A third may change an allocation because recent market performance has become unusually influential.

The economic choice remains. What changes is our understanding of the person making it.

This becomes important when individual choices are aggregated. Microeconomics often begins with individual decision makers, but markets are created through the interaction of many of those decisions. The same principle applies to stocks. A single investor deciding that a company is undervalued means little to the broader market. When many investors reach that conclusion and commit capital, their combined demand becomes economically significant.

Behavioral influences can aggregate in the same way. If one investor becomes unusually optimistic after a period of strong returns, the market effect is negligible. If large numbers of investors become more optimistic and increase their allocations, the result can affect demand and capital flows. The psychological influence has become part of a market outcome because it changed enough economic decisions.

This does not mean we can observe a rising stock price and conclude that behavioral bias caused it. Price changes can reflect new information about earnings, interest rates, economic growth, competition, technology, or countless other factors. The difficulty is that behavioral and fundamental explanations can operate simultaneously.

Suppose a company announces stronger-than-expected earnings. Investors reasonably increase their expectations about future profitability, and the stock rises. That initial movement can be justified by new information. The rising price then attracts additional attention. Investors who missed the first increase begin purchasing shares. Funds with exposure to the company report stronger performance and attract additional capital. Other managers increase their exposure because the stock has become more important to relative performance.

The original economic information has not disappeared. But the response to that information has created additional behavior.

This is one reason behavioral economics is valuable as an extension of microeconomic analysis. It allows us to examine the path between an economic event and the eventual market outcome rather than assuming that all participants respond to information in the same way.

The same reasoning applies to market declines. Weak earnings may justify a lower valuation. The resulting decline can then influence risk perceptions, investor withdrawals, institutional positioning, and expectations about what other participants will do next. The eventual market movement may reflect both the original information and the responses that followed it.

Market outcomes are therefore produced through interaction. Prices provide signals and incentives, but people interpret those signals. Their interpretations become decisions, and their decisions can affect the prices everyone else observes.

# Strategic Interaction Between Market Participants

The behavior of other people matters in financial markets because investors are not making choices in isolation. A decision can depend partly on what the investor expects someone else to do.

This introduces **strategic interaction** into the market.

Consider a portfolio manager who believes a stock is expensive. If the only question were the manager's estimate of fundamental value, avoiding the stock might appear straightforward. But suppose the stock represents a large portion of the manager's benchmark and continues rising as other institutions purchase it. Avoiding the stock can create increasing relative underperformance.

The manager now has to consider more than valuation. The behavior of other market participants affects the consequences of the decision.

Retail investors face their own version of this problem. Someone may believe the broader market has become expensive but hesitate to sell because prices could continue rising for years. Another investor may want to purchase a rapidly rising stock because they expect additional buyers to continue pushing the price higher.

In both cases, the investor is thinking about other investors.

This connects behavioral economics with ideas from game theory. A **strategic decision** is one in which the best choice can depend partly on the choices made by others. Financial markets contain many situations with this characteristic because market participants continually form expectations about one another.

Suppose an investor becomes concerned about a potential market decline but believes most other investors will remain confident. Selling immediately may cause the investor to miss additional gains. If the investor instead believes everyone else is about to sell, waiting becomes much less attractive.

The underlying securities could be identical in both situations. What changed was the investor's expectation about other people's behavior.

Liquidity makes this interaction especially important. An investor may be comfortable owning an asset while believing there will always be other participants willing to trade it. If the investor begins expecting many people to sell simultaneously, the value placed on liquidity can increase quickly.

The investor may then decide to sell before everyone else does.

If enough investors reach the same conclusion, the expectation can contribute to the outcome itself.

People sell because they expect other people to sell, and their selling creates exactly the market pressure they anticipated.

The opposite can occur during rallies. Investors may purchase an asset partly because they expect continued demand from other investors. Rising prices appear to confirm the expectation, encouraging participants to remain in the market.

This does not require investors to ignore fundamental value. A portfolio manager can simultaneously have an opinion about what an asset is worth and an expectation about how other market participants will behave. Those two beliefs may even point in different directions.

Institutional and retail investors also respond to each other indirectly. Retail investors may watch institutional activity as a signal of professional conviction. Institutions may monitor retail sentiment, trading activity, fund flows, and market momentum. Asset owners evaluate investment managers, while investment managers anticipate how asset owners may respond to periods of underperformance.

The result is a network of strategic relationships rather than two completely separate groups.

This perspective also helps explain why incentives matter so much. A decision that appears irrational when viewed only through the expected return of an asset may become more understandable when we include the reactions of other participants.

A manager staying relatively close to a benchmark may be responding to career risk. An asset owner moving capital after prolonged underperformance may be responding to governance responsibilities. A retail investor holding more liquidity during a period of uncertainty may value financial flexibility more than maximum expected return.

Behavioral economics should not be used to label every unusual decision as a mistake. Sometimes the apparent irrationality disappears once the full incentive structure is understood.

Strategic interaction makes that distinction particularly important because investors are making decisions inside a market populated by other decision makers. What someone else does can change the payoff associated with your own choice.

## What Behavioral Economics Can and Cannot Explain About Markets

Behavioral economics is powerful because it gives us concepts for understanding parts of financial decision making that a perfectly rational model can overlook. It can help explain why losses may influence people differently from equivalent gains, why previous prices remain psychologically important, why recent events can dominate expectations, why investors sometimes follow other investors, and why professional expertise does not completely remove behavioral influences.

But behavioral economics also has limits.

It cannot tell us that every market rally is a bubble. It cannot tell us that every crash is caused by panic. It cannot tell us that retail investors are irrational or that institutional investors are rational. It cannot automatically tell us whether a particular stock is overvalued or undervalued.

Most importantly, identifying a behavioral tendency after an event does not necessarily mean that tendency caused the event.

Suppose investors sell during a recession. Loss aversion may be present, but investors may also be responding rationally to declining corporate earnings and increasing economic risk. If credit conditions are deteriorating and businesses are failing, falling asset prices do not require a psychological explanation.

The behavioral question concerns how people respond to those economic conditions.

Did investors react more strongly because recent losses changed their perception of risk? Did widespread selling become social information for other investors? Did fund outflows place additional pressure on institutions? Did institutional responses contribute to further market activity?

Those questions add depth to the economic analysis without requiring behavior to explain everything.

The same caution applies to bubbles. Rising prices, enthusiasm, social proof, and FOMO can contribute to speculative behavior, but strong price appreciation can also reflect genuine changes in economic value. A new technology can transform an industry. A company can grow faster than expected. Lower interest rates can change asset valuations. Investors can be optimistic and correct.

Behavioral explanations are most useful when they help us understand the decisions connecting these economic developments to market outcomes.

There is another limitation. Behavioral tendencies do not always tell us what someone will do.

Loss aversion does not mean every investor will hold a losing stock. Some investors will sell quickly because they fear an even larger loss. Herd behavior does not mean everyone follows the crowd. Some investors deliberately take positions against prevailing sentiment. Recency does not mean investors completely ignore long-term evidence.

Human behavior varies.

Institutions vary too. A hedge fund, pension fund, mutual fund, insurance company, and endowment may respond very differently to the same market conditions because their objectives and constraints are different.

This makes behavioral economics better suited to explaining tendencies and patterns than producing simple predictions about exactly what the market will do next.

Knowing that investors can become overconfident does not tell us when a market will peak. Knowing that fear can contribute to selling does not tell us where a market decline will end. Knowing that capital flows can reinforce market activity does not tell us whether the next inflow will cause prices to rise.

Financial markets remain uncertain because countless participants are responding to changing information while also responding to one another.

That uncertainty is not a weakness of the behavioral approach. It is part of the reason the approach is useful.

A model can simplify the investor so that economic relationships are easier to understand. Behavioral economics reminds us that the actual investor remains a human being operating in an environment where information is incomplete, outcomes are uncertain, incentives differ, and other people's decisions matter.

The strongest understanding of financial markets therefore does not require choosing between traditional economics and behavioral economics. Traditional economic concepts help explain incentives, scarcity, opportunity costs, prices, risk, and resource allocation. Behavioral economics helps explain how people perceive and respond to those conditions.

Together, they provide a more complete view of market decision making.

## Last Thoughts

Behavioral economics gives us a way to connect individual decision making with broader financial market outcomes without treating psychology as a replacement for economics. Investors still respond to incentives, prices, risk, opportunity costs, and changing economic conditions, but they interpret those conditions through expectations, experiences, reference points, and observations of other market participants. Strategic interaction adds another layer because the consequences of one investor's decision can depend partly on what others decide to do. When these decisions occur across retail investors, asset owners, investment managers, and other institutions, individual behavior can become capital flows and market activity. Behavioral economics cannot explain every price movement or predict exactly what markets will do next. What it can do is help us understand how the decisions of real people move through a financial system, interact with the decisions of others, and sometimes become part of the market outcomes everyone is trying to understand.

# Last Thoughts

Financial markets are often described through prices, returns, earnings, interest rates, valuations, and economic indicators. These measurements are necessary because they allow us to observe what is happening across markets. Yet throughout this book, we have approached those numbers from another direction. Behind changes in prices and movements of capital are decisions made by people. Those people may be investing their own savings, managing a mutual fund, allocating pension assets, running a hedge fund, or making decisions inside a large financial institution. The size and purpose of the capital may change, but human decision making remains part of the process.

## Markets as Systems of Human Interaction

One of the most useful ways to think about the stock market is as a system of interacting participants rather than a single entity making decisions. There is no one person deciding what the market believes a company is worth. Prices emerge from the interaction of buyers and sellers who may have very different expectations, objectives, information, incentives, and time horizons.

This helps explain why behavioral economics belongs within a broader economic discussion of financial markets. Traditional economic concepts remain important. Investors face scarcity because capital is limited. They make tradeoffs because allocating money to one investment means giving up another opportunity. They respond to incentives, evaluate risk, and attempt to make choices that serve their objectives.

Behavioral economics adds the recognition that these decisions are made by people who do not always interpret information in the same way.

An investor can become concerned about a loss because the current value of a portfolio has fallen below an important reference point. Another investor can look at the same decline and see an opportunity. A portfolio manager may believe an asset is attractive while still worrying about the consequences of short-term underperformance. An asset owner may believe in a long-term strategy while becoming uncomfortable after several years of disappointing results.

These participants are observing the same market, but they are not experiencing the same decision.

That difference matters because markets require disagreement. A person selling a stock needs someone willing to buy it. The buyer and seller can observe the same price and reach different conclusions about what should happen next.

Behavioral economics does not remove this diversity by claiming that everyone responds to the same bias in the same way. Instead, it helps explain why perceptions and decisions can differ even when people are responding to similar information.

The market then brings those decisions together.

A change in expectations can alter demand. A change in perceived risk can influence an allocation. A loss can cause an investor to withdraw capital. Strong performance can attract new money. Institutional managers can respond to changing flows, while asset owners can respond to manager performance.

Each decision enters a system containing other decision makers.

That is what makes financial markets particularly interesting from a behavioral perspective. People do not simply react to economic conditions. They also react to a market that is being continuously shaped by the reactions of other people.

## Individual Decisions, Institutional Responses, and Collective Outcomes

The relationship between individual and institutional investors has been central to this book because it demonstrates how behavior can move through different levels of the financial system.

A retail investor deciding to move money into a mutual fund is making an individual allocation decision. The investor does not determine which securities the fund will purchase, but the decision changes where capital is being managed. If many investors make similar decisions, the resulting inflows can become significant.

The investment manager then operates within the new capital conditions. The manager decides how the available money should be allocated according to the fund's strategy, mandate, liquidity needs, and assessment of investment opportunities.

The process can work in reverse. Investors withdraw money, the fund experiences outflows, and the manager responds to those changing conditions.

Asset owners can create similar relationships at a much larger scale. A pension fund, endowment, or other asset owner can move substantial amounts of money between investment managers or strategies. Those allocation decisions can change the amount of capital institutions have available to deploy.

This is where individual decisions can begin contributing to **collective outcomes**.

The connection does not mean every dollar entering a fund immediately causes a stock purchase or every withdrawal immediately causes a sale. Financial institutions manage liquidity and portfolios in different ways. The relationship is more important than any simple mechanical rule.

People supplying capital can affect the environment facing the people managing capital.

The people managing capital can then affect the market environment facing the people supplying it.

Suppose investors become increasingly optimistic after a long period of strong returns. More capital moves toward investments that have recently performed well. Institutions receiving that capital make portfolio decisions. Market activity contributes to the prices and returns that investors observe.

Those results become part of the next decision.

The process can continue as long as enough participants continue responding in ways that reinforce it.

During a downturn, the direction can change. Falling prices create losses. Losses alter expectations and perceptions of risk. Some investors withdraw capital. Institutions respond to changing flows and market conditions. Selling activity can contribute to further declines, which become new information for other investors.

This is the interaction between behavior and capital that makes behavioral economics particularly relevant to financial markets.

It also explains why we should be careful about dividing investors into simple categories of rational and irrational participants.

Retail investors can make carefully reasoned decisions. Institutional investors can experience behavioral biases. A fund manager can respond rationally to an incentive that appears irrational to someone who does not face the same constraint. An investor can follow a crowd because the crowd contains useful information, while another investor can follow the same crowd without independently considering why everyone is moving in that direction.

The transaction alone does not always reveal the reasoning behind it.

Understanding market behavior therefore requires more than observing who bought and who sold. We have to consider the incentives, expectations, constraints, and information surrounding those decisions.

## A Broader View of Investor and Market Behavior

Behavioral economics is sometimes reduced to a collection of biases. Loss aversion, anchoring, overconfidence, recency, herd behavior, and other concepts are useful, but memorizing a list of behavioral tendencies misses the larger point.

The more important idea is that economic decisions are made by human beings.

Those decisions occur within systems.

In financial markets, the system includes retail investors, institutional investors, asset owners, investment managers, corporations, financial intermediaries, and many other participants. Each has different objectives and constraints, yet their decisions can affect one another through prices and capital flows.

This broader view also prevents behavioral economics from becoming an explanation for everything that happens in the stock market.

A market decline is not automatically evidence of panic. Investors may be responding to deteriorating earnings, higher interest rates, tighter credit conditions, weaker economic growth, or a genuine increase in financial risk. A rally is not automatically evidence of irrational enthusiasm. Prices can rise because expected profits improve or because economic conditions become more favorable.

Behavioral economics becomes useful when we ask how people respond to those developments.

A change in interest rates is an economic event. How investors interpret that change is a behavioral question. A decline in corporate earnings changes financial expectations. How quickly investors react, how strongly they respond, and how much they rely on the behavior of others can involve behavioral considerations.

The two forms of analysis can exist together.

This is also why behavioral economics should not be treated as a method for predicting the stock market. Knowing that investors experience loss aversion does not tell us when a market will crash. Recognizing herd behavior does not tell us when a rally will end. Understanding that recent performance can influence expectations does not reveal tomorrow's stock prices.

Human behavior can help explain market dynamics without making those dynamics predictable.

The stock market contains too many participants, incentives, changing conditions, and competing expectations for one behavioral principle to determine every outcome. Even when a behavioral tendency is present, different investors may respond to it differently.

That uncertainty is part of the market itself.

What behavioral economics gives us is a richer framework for thinking about what happens between information and action. Economic information enters the market, people interpret it, decisions are made, capital moves, and the resulting market activity becomes information for another round of decisions.

The relationship is continuous.

That perspective also brings us back to the connection between microeconomics and financial markets. A large market movement can begin with decisions that are individually small. Each person responds to incentives, constraints, expectations, and preferences. Institutions do the same within more complex organizational structures. When enough of those decisions interact, the aggregate result can become economically significant.

A market rally, a wave of fund inflows, a shift toward cash, or a period of intense selling may appear to be a single event when viewed from a distance. Up close, each consists of many separate decisions.

Behavioral economics helps us examine the people making them.

## Last Thoughts

The stock market is both an economic system and a human system. Prices, valuations, earnings, interest rates, liquidity, and capital remain fundamental to understanding financial markets, but none of these eliminates the role of the people deciding how money should be allocated. Retail investors respond to gains, losses, information, expectations, and the behavior of others. Institutional investors operate with greater resources while facing their own mandates, benchmarks, incentives, and professional pressures. Asset owners decide where large pools of capital should be managed, and investment managers decide how that capital should be deployed. These decisions interact through capital flows and market prices, creating a system in which investor behavior can become market behavior and market behavior can influence investors in return. Behavioral economics does not give us a simple explanation for every rally, bubble, downturn, or crash. It gives us something more useful: a framework for examining how human decisions interact with economic forces and how, when enough of those decisions come together, they can become part of the movement of the market itself.

## About the Author

Roggie "Raj" Clark is an entrepreneur and a 10-year marketing professional with a proven track record in e-commerce and digital business growth. Having built and managed successful online stores with thousands of sales and consulted for numerous marketing clients, Roggie has mastered the intricacies of online marketing, branding, and consumer behavior. He has also written several popular books on digital marketing, SEO (search engine optimization), and programming (HTML, CSS, and JavaScript).

As a former marketing manager at a fintech company—a role he secured through his own marketing and financial expertise—Roggie gained firsthand experience in financial strategy and wealth-building. This journey inspired him to share insights with amateur investors, helping them save money, make smarter financial decisions, and build long-term wealth. Raj currently lives in Maryland with his sister and niece.